A Case for

Fascism

𝕸𝖍𝖆𝖙 𝖎𝖘 𝕱𝖆𝖘𝖈𝖎𝖘𝖒?

"Fascism is not a philosophy in the ordinary sense of the term, and still less is it a religion. It is also not an explicated and definitive political doctrine, articulated in a series of formulae." – **Giovanni Gentile**

What is fascism? It seems like simple enough of a question, hell everyone knows what Fascism is, it's that thing you don't like; it's bossy, demanding, restrictive, racist, and oppressive. It could mean so many things, all depending on the accuser's *self-defined* definition.

"Fascist" has become an abstract slander that seems to imply the person being called a "Fascist" is in some way the oppressor of the accusing party. Therefore it is easy for opposing ends of the limited modern political spectrum to accuse each other of being *Fascist*. The "Right" will call the liberal "Left" "Fascist" and the "Left" will call the conservative "Right" "Fascist"; accordingly the Libertarian deems them both Fascist. Meanwhile all parties and people who toss around the *"you're a Fascist"* accusation couldn't be further from the truth, as there exists no political Fascist in the world of modern politics, and no Fascist parties in the modern political spectrum.

When there is no one to speak up for the Fascist philosophy in the public stage it can be no wonder that the term 'Fascist' has become merely an abstract physiological tool used for slander. Since *History is* indeed *written by the victors*, the ideal of Fascism has been reduced to simple totalitarianism in the Democratic West. Dictators, fiction and non-fiction, are often, if not always, portrayed as cartoonish, evil, power hungry lunatics that derive their only pleasures in life from the meaningless mass murder of innocent civilians.

With public education, mass media, and pop culture all simplifying and demonizing Fascism most people go through life merely scratching the surface of what it is to be a Fascist. We are told we live in the 'free-ist" part of the world, where our political system allows free flowing conversation and a true exchange of ideas; tolerance, and sometimes even media promotion of ideologies that embrace the extremes of the modern Right-Left political spectrum like Libertarianism and Communism, are presented as proofs of our "free" political system. But what of

Fascism? Something that is neither Right nor left but rather the preverbal Middle. Where is the tolerance for the Fascist ideal? Where is the free flowing conversation and exchange of ideas? It does not exist.

While the individualism of the Libertarians may be an extreme section of the right wing ideology it is still essentially an extension of the right; the same can be said for the extreme collectivism of the modern neo-Marxist being an extension of the Left. Fascism on the other hand is the revolutionary middle; politics that magnifies neither the Right nor Left, but is a monolith unto itself; A true 3rd position that uses individualism to promote and enhance collectivism.

The Fascist philosophy seeks to find a reasonable middle ground in the right-left political spectrum. At the root of the Fascist philosophy is the understanding that: *UNITED WE ARE STRONGER.*

Even in man's most primitive form it was quickly understood: that the tribes whose members worked together not only survived but thrived. They grew from small tribes to villages-towns-cities-nations; working together, growing together, and advancing together.

The etymology of Fascism can be seen in the understanding that a single stick could be easily broken, but a fascio (bundle) could not. And from this most basic of foundations Fascism builds its obelisk. Understanding people with common goals were an untied people, and a united people could achieve the unimaginable.

The Fascist thought is a living ideal in the sense that every thought, like every person, every animal, and every plant is cosmically intertwined and organic. Forever growing and evolving, not sedentary and decaying like the Right – Left paradigm, that while slightly redefining it's self time-to-time, always ensures a heated divide and deliberate disharmony between the citizens.

Our awareness to self and surrounding are ever growing and expanding as too is the Fascist thought of taking what exists and creating the fantastical: A realization of great visions and collective goals fueled by the common desire to understand and prosper during this relatively short time on Earth.

Jaded by materialism and extreme individualism the idea of a common good and a great goal has long since lost its luster with the people, being written off as unattainable, unworthy, or simply unrealistic. Dismissed from the possibility of reality, the *common good* is now scoffed at by the people it would enrich the most. And the lack of unified goals leaves mankind running around like chickens with their heads cut off, running to and from work and play, only pausing momentarily to admire in awe the latest upgrade in technology that makes his or her life easier and more complacent.

The Integral nature of the Fascist philosophy serves as the cracks and crevasses the climber uses to pull him upwards towards the light of a new day. Armed with a new perspective of life the Fascist approaches the problems of modernity and existence as wonderful challenges with solvable problems, not stresses piled one on top another with no end in sight and always weighing heavy on one's conscious.

Fascism does seek fantastical goals because the strength of united man is unsurpassed in all living things on this Earth. The Fascist loves the idea of *united man* but distrusts man by himself.

Man can be lead astray by himself, but man unified is supported, and lifted, by his brothers, by the common good - by the unified goals of his society.

A common mission towards a greater ideal binds men together stronger than anything created in the world of capital lust and gluttony. When man has no purpose he becomes a self-destructive wreck, living his one life away in nihilist hedonism… Life is reduced to mere pleasure seeking consuming and measuring one's worth through material accumulation. Living and dying a whole life cycle without ever addressing the questions of 'why' and 'how' instead living in ignorant bliss, servant to those that pray on your lower instincts, and seek to suppress your higher-self. And like any good servant you remain loyal to your masters, or develop Stockholm syndrome for them. You even learn to speak their language as you brag about your "liberty" and "freedom" all the meanwhile being a slave to yourself...And it's not even you, it's the *'you'* that they created with their advertisements, their institutional learning facilities, their means of mass communication.

Molding a *'you'* at your lowest potential. Not high enough to demand more of life, but not so low enough to not be able to be a functioning and appreciative cog in the wheel. Capitalism is man's prolonged suicide.

Fascism seeks a *'you'* of your highest potential... Fit of mind and body, in control of your passions. The high aspirations of a united society are only attainable when the people, both collectively and individually, are of the best quality possible.

When life is lived for the pursuit of capital, men are reduced to mere commodities In contrast when life is lived for the pursuit of great goals men are integral components. Fascism is the philosophy of the great goal.

Pillars of Fascism

"Unity is the first degree of Fascism, the prerequisite of achievement. Whenever and wherever men and women band together, sinking all personal prejudice and ambition, for the attainment of a common goal, for the fulfillment of a common ideal, there is a fasces in being."- **Jorian Jenks**

The Fascist philosophy has been around for a very long time and practiced in numerous different countries. Each flavor of Fascism has always differed country to country and culture to culture. Despite the diversity of international Fascism, there always remain a few pillars that are essentially mandatory in building a Fascist society; these pillars are in-deed what make Fascism-Fascism, and not any other form of collectivist government.

United Man

First and foremost is: *United Man*: a united people
are detrimental to a successful Fascist society. With
a governmental system that sets National goals and
works towards a common good, a harmonious
population is mandatory if the Nation hopes to grow
and prosper. General unity in all aspects of public
life: politics, social, and financial is essential. Division
of the masses over political and social issues is
downright cancerous to a collective society. The
vitality of a Nation is in its citizens; for that reason
the Nation and the people who represent the Nation
cannot exist in a sea of discord. Modern Democracy
on the other hand encourages the rift among its
citizenry. People are divided by the right-left political
spectrum; urban and rural areas; religion and non-
religion, conflicting sub-cultures and so on... In
Fascism people are unified through the common
good: the successes or failures of a Nation impact
everyone in society, from the street cleaner to the
brain surgeon. All people are integral in the
development of the Fascist nation.

Anything is obtainable by a truly unified people. The power of a motivated unified people with a sense of purpose is unmatched in Nature. The biggest crime committed by modern day Democracy is not only encouraging division of the people but even portraying the division as its greatest virtue!

Nationalism

Fascism is solely Nationalistic,   As opposed to Communism, and International Capitalism which both strive to achieve a vapidness of individual cultures, either through force, or commercialism. Modern Democracy fills people's heads with the tale of *liberating the world*, in reality: an Iron fisted control by wealthy peoples over the less fortunate takes place with imposed *universal laws* forcefully destroying the natural diversity of life. For man to be unified as much is possible he must have commonalities in culture and common goals with his fellow citizens. These commonalities are obtained, preserved and progressed within the framework of the Nation. Nation-hood is a means of preserving a culture, and people - which in turns ensures the best advances towards true unity. Every country would benefit under their own Nationalism, and of course every country can be different but respect each other - work together to advance together; truly diverse in culture, tradition, and ethnicity but unified in a universal common good of self and world progress. Both Democracy and Communism seek to convert the world to 'their' way of life...*By any means necessary.*

National Goals

In the Fascist political structure collective goals for society are set, ranging from anything to do with: structure, architecture, terraforming, science, exploration, education, spirituality etc... Compare the concept of National goals to the modern concepts of Liberal Democracies where the goals are not unified, but very individual, and the goal is: the obtainment of as much capital as possible. Capital which in turn is used to consume material trinkets. Instead of allowing blind greed to dictate the course of the people, a well thought-out, debated, and finalized course is set by knowledgeable men who are entrusted through merit, to coordinate the means and methods of successfully obtaining collective goals. These goals may be as scientific and daring as exploring our universe or as pragmatic and needed as building our infrastructure. Whatever they may be they bring us together and give us greater purpose. As it is today: valuable resources are hoarded by a *select few* and dispensed as they deem fit. And what they deem fit is to continue the system of a divided citizenry all individually pursuing capital. This keeps the power in the *selected few's* hands. Resources should be used to advance society as a whole; a person's motivation should not be 'division and pursuit of capital' but rather unity and pursuit of advancement.

Onearchy

A principle philosophy of Fascist thought is: *Thought & Action*. A room full of squabbling old men and women with conflicting interests, and price tags on their votes is by no means what is thought of when one thinks of the manner a people progress together.

One leader entrusted with the final decision. The people: intellectuals, philosophers, scientists, blue collar workers, white collar workers etc... Guide and support, as the base of a pyramid supports the very top of the point, the leader, in decision making and the final word is truly the tip of the spear being thrusted forward. Which also means failure, or tyranny have only one person to blame. The buck truly starts and stops with the figure head of the people. A leader takes extreme ownership of his decisions and their results. The Fascist dictator is by no means a monarchy but rather a meritocracy; leaders chosen because of ability not bloodlines, or wealth. A brief synopsis of historical rule shows us: The god-kings were replaced by the kings blessed by god, and nobility; those nobles blessed by god were replaced by the merchants who rule today. There has always been a ruler, whether behind a curtain or right in front of your face. The beauty of the leader being one person, the quintessential spear tip of the nation, is that the buck stops with him. If things are going bad, or corruption has run amuck the leader take full responsibility. There are no two-ways about it: A healthy society will demand and enforce a healthy leader. A healthy people will also not tolerate tyranny, abuse of power, or continual failure.

Government oversight and/or control over mass industry and mass media

Mass industry, and media are over kept by the state, ensuring the needs of a people are met. Over and under production are avoided, or at least an attempt to avoid such things; the state meditates between workers and owners when problems arise. The economy becomes a well calculated equation that exists to serve and advance people. As opposed to heartless Capitalism which only underlying concern is profit. Instead of an attempt at a calculated direction of economy it is *dog eat dog*, and brotherhood takes a backseat to *figures*. Misuse of man can be seen through-out the whole American Liberal Capitalist Democracy... First the Irish and other non-WASP Europeans, followed by Africans... When man moved away from slavery, the wage slave came into existence, recently the illegal Mexican immigrant population has heavily filled this role, and only to slowly be replaced by machines... What of the people of the American Nation? The citizen is tossed aside for capital... Industry gutted, small business stamped out, and farms bankrupt; monopoly and oligarchy orgies in vogue. Capitalism is cancerous. It cares not for your wellbeing. Communism reduces you, or even (in some sad cases) elevates you to the 'standard'. Oversight is a reality no matter what; it is only the perception of oversight that changes. Shall elite merchants have that oversight? Or Honorable brothers and sisters motivated by the *common good* and National advancement? To allow people who only care for profit to run our media and Government while telling us *'there is no oversight'* or *collusion* is to be the lamb listening to the sweet melody being sung gently in its ear right before the blade rips across its throat. Since <u>no matter what</u> oversight will exist (in one form or another) it simply makes more sense to have people with their citizens' best interest at heart in charge of that oversight.

Meritocracy

True equal opportunity for man is created in the Fascist structure. Schooling made available to everyone; the same level of education regardless of class, wealth, birth etc... Advancement through one's actions and results. The communist says *we are all equal despite results!* The modern Democracy says *we all have equal opportunity, but people with more money just have more of an equal opportunity.* The Fascist says *we all have the same starting point and may we all finish where we are best suited.* No quotas to fill or better schools for the rich; each child is given the best education as possible and are encouraged to seek career pursuits where they are best skilled and interested. To cultivate a people that excel at their task there must be true equal starting point; to enhance competition, so we know, without doubt the people best suited to do so are elevated to do so. Alongside Nationalization of Education is the Nationalization of Healthcare: wealth should not determine how much we care for our fellow citizen, and only a sick detached people could think otherwise.

Common Misnomers Of Fascism

"Anyone who has declared someone else to be an idiot, a bad apple, is annoyed when it turns out in the end that he isn't."- **Friedrich Nietzsche**

In Fascism there is no free speech

There is no actual thing as "free speech", no matter the society all speech is, and has always been open to consequences. The same holds true for Fascist society. Debate on policy, philosophy, and direction of government has always played a vital part in Fascism and always will. On the other hand purposely spreading public discontent in the people has always typically been suppressed. A fine line is drawn between healthy debate, and confrontational attacks intended to derail the course. "Free Speech" is an abstract tool used to befuddle us. Nothing in this life is Free, for every action there is a re-action. The same people today who proselytize "Free Speech" are the same people that will demand your being fired from a job because you may have used a 'word' that has been negatively stigmatized. Their hypocrisy and illogic seemingly have no bounds. I would suspect speech under Fascist America will be a lot more founded in reality than speech is today. If government doesn't lock you up - you will lose your job - or somebody will punch you in the face - murder you - slash your tires...So on and so on... There is always consequence for what you say; do not let them fool you into servitude with these abstract concepts like "Free Speech".

Fascist are all racist

Often enough we are told that Fascism is racist and we are shown clips of Nazis marching, to enforce the image of a totalitarian racist regime, whose sole purpose is to oppress and even murder those who do not look like them! This is a ludicrous claim and the only people who believe it are the people who do not take time to verify the claim. If they did take the small amount of time required they would see that Nazi Germany was just one brand, out of many Fascist brands... In fact, Nazi Germany was the only brand to start off as a "racist" brand of Fascism. (in fact Germany wasn't even racist in the manner it is promoted by the American media, their racialism was not an international racism, wanting to do harm to different races outside of Germany, but a national one, and that wasn't even as draconian as claimed with measures like the 1/4th law) so even the racism of Germany is over dramatized by the mass media, and American public education. Now it is true that Italy later adapted race laws but this was inspired by Hitler and not organic in Italian fascism. Mussolini So outside of Germany, every other fascist brand put the idea of the nation above that of biological race.. Germany was the exception, not the rule.

(English Fascist) Mosley says:

"It is utterly untrue that the British Union is largely a racialist movement. ...For as its followers are fervent believers in the Empire, and as the empire contains scores of races, to be anti any one race is a contradiction in terms. If the Jews place Jewry first, we are against them; but if they place Britain first they have nothing to fear. And the same applies to all other races, cults, and creeds."

(Spanish Fascist) Jose Antonio Primo de Rivera:

"Here is what is required by our total sense of the Patra and the state which is to serve it: That is all the people of Spain, however diverse they may be, feel in harmony with an irrevocable unity of destiny."

"National Socialism is preoccupied by the body (namely the racial eugenics) whereas Legionarism is preoccupied by something much deeper: by the

soul." ---The Nest Leader's manual (Romanian Fascists)

Whether it was the Brazilian Integralists or the National Socialist Movement of Chile... it did not matter, the common theme was society first... Fascism is not only a political philosophy built around unity, but also meritocracies. The worth of a man through deed, not just fitting a certain biological background.

Because Fascism is not racist in nature, does not mean it is egalitarian... Egalitarianism is a lie told by Democracy and Communism. Since both political philosophies reduce men to simple numbers, the facade of equality strips the individual of both his unique spirit, and his racial soul. Pretending biological differences in races does not exist- helps no one, and only causes more conflict; it's a belief based on a lie. People are so used to being divided, and pushed to their own extremes they think only racism or egalitarianism can exist, but as Fascism is politics in moderation so is being a race realist. We as Americans are diverse, there are those in power that seek to end the diversity by pushing forward agendas to mix the races and create a *universal tan man*...A cosmopolitan creation with no roots, therefore easily controlled and materialist. Making them obedient workers to Communism and/or Capitalism.

The thought that in America the races cannot work towards common goals, while maintaining their genetic lineage, their cultural traditions, and their unique racial expression is a thought manufactured by the global elite who benefit from the concept of the "melting pot": the person with no identity except the one he purchase at the store.

Today, in America, we are at a crossroads and the paths of the future are either Communism, with its pretty lies, and suppression of the human will, or Fascism with its rationality and encouragement of the human will. The belief that we can only co-exist by genetically wiping each out is a false belief. The American Fascist knows we can be diverse and unified in our common goals and shared destiny. We are different as individuals, races, ethnicities, religions...etc...But we are unified in our citizenship and our belief in the common good. As different as we may be, our common destiny is our true unifying factor that obliterates all petty division.

Fascist are religious zealots

Much like the racism aspect, religions or lack thereof depend on the individual party. Some Fascist parties have been heavily Christian; other used the political ideology as their religion... It can be said Fascist philosophy embraces spiritualism, a profound interest and awe of the unknown and supernatural...So therefore not atheistic, but not universally in support of a specific religion as well, truly secular. Religion or non-religion is separate from government. What someone believes or disbelieves is up to them as individuals, not for the state to persuade or decide.

Fascism is war like and murderous

Man is *war like and murderous*. Murder, war, slavery, hate, etc... Exist in man, and has existed in every form of government man has created, present day included. No form of government is more murderous than the other by itself. Some people, leaders, eras have been bloodier than the next, but any political system by itself cannot be credited with being more violent then the next. To suggest so is pure hyperbole. Fascism is a philosophy and like any form of government: a tool for man to use. Sometimes war happens, sometimes peace does. We prefer peace, but will not hesitate to defend ourselves. With the same intensity the Fascist loves his fellow citizen is the same intensity he attacks his enemy with. No one governmental philosophy has a monopoly of murder. There is enough to go around for every system to share in the blame.

Fascism kills individual freedom, competition, and creativity.

Fascism is not Communism. Competition exists, and is in fact encouraged (Fascism is meritocracy afterall). All salaries are not the same, but the gap between top and bottom wage earners are no longer monstrous: *the sky is not endless and the pit bottomless.* Individual freedoms typically have remained as they are today. Fascism promotes and maybe even enforces a common decency when interacting in public settings but by no means, on a whole, seeks to micro-manage morality: *what you do in your house is your business.* Just because the motivation of man is not solely reduced to personal greed does not mean individual freedom all of sudden does not exist...We are men...Not ants, it is in our nature to be who we are and blaze a trail. To both conform and unconform. Individuality and personal incentive has not been eradicated, but rather rearranged to *common good* ahead of personal profit. Something that cannot be measured in numbers; something much more fulfilling. Fascists are not fool enough to think they can change human nature (like Communism). Instead Fascism changes the motivation from 'pursuit of capital' to pursuit of individual and collective advancement.

Thought & Action

"Like all sound political conceptions, Fascism is action and it is thought; action in which doctrine is immanent"- **Benito Mussolini**

Fascism is reactionary in the sense: it is always revolutionary. Fascism always rises as a response of the people with the intent on smashing decadent political institutions that have run unchecked for too long and no longer holds the people and state in esteem. Or as a reaction to Marxism whenever it threatens to obtain power.

One, among many, of the revolutionary concepts of Fascism is *Thought and Action*; plucking ideas from the metaphysical and transforming them into physical world tangible realities, bringing ideas to life. These *living ideas* are almost impossible in liberal democracies.

When society is set up in a pyramid basis: with the broad mass supporting the base, getting thinner as it reaches the tip (leader). Decisions put into action by the leader.

The ideas of our most gifted thinkers (scientist, philosophers, etc.) not sidelined by cooperate interest but boldly put into action.

In modern democracy, a "thought" must go through a long difficult process to becoming a reality. Most damning is not the process itself but the people involved, for first you have a group of law makers who are divided politically, and then you have to factor in corporate interests. If the "thought" can get passed the political division, and the corporate intrusion and the political action committees (PAC) then finally it has a chance to surface into reality...*If the media allows it.*

With this long drawn out process with so many conflicting views it is no wonder, so few great ideas ever see the light of day, or receive the proper attention and funding.

We as a society essentially have been spinning our wheels in the mud.

Fascism is action orientated once the Thought is put through it must be put into Action. We actually seek (as a unified people) to make our dreams real.

Modernity...What have you done for us lately?

"The man who never looked into a newspaper is better informed than he who reads them, inasmuch as he who knows nothing is nearer to the truth than he whose mind is filled with half-truths and errors." – **Thomas Jefferson**

Modern Liberal Democracy sold us the lie that once we got rid of the Feudal System and Authoritarianism we also got rid of an uncaring aristocracy. This is not the truth; what happened was not that the aristocracy was done away with altogether, but rather it morphed into the hands of a different class: The merchant class.

In the past the people in society who had the high positions of power, influence, and control i.e. the Nobility. The Nobility (depending on the governmental structure) was typically made up of people who were either blood born into a noble family (monarchy), or through either their own intelligence, cunning, or courageousness moved themselves up the social ladder (merit).

Today, our Nobility is the merchant and lawyer class...Money and rhetoric has become the dominating factors that ascend someone to the modern aristocracy. Our current day government is filled with lawyers, who use their skills in rhetoric to pander, connive, and hoodwink their way into governmental power. The most successful merchants (be they Bankers, or CEO's of multi-National companies) in turn buy the lawyers, both as they run for office, or in office, thus ensuring *their* interests are taken care of by the lawyer class... often enough *their* interests conflict with *ours.* So, while the *'Lawyers'* that run for office tell us 'they run for office out of a desire to serve us', we see by their deeds - that they truly run for office to serve (1) Themselves and in turn (2) The merchants filling their pockets with cash.

But who can blame them? This is what Capitalism encourages... Instead of being fellow citizens, (brothers and sisters) we are all individual competitors. For example If my neighbor works for a rival company, let's say a car manufacturing company; The more cars his company sells, the less the company I work for will sell, which means I could be out of a job, and not provide for my family...But if on the other hand his company goes out of business, that just ensures my company will be able to sell more cars, thus giving me job security to provide for my family; so now I openly root for the down fall of my neighbor, because his fall is my rise. We are no longer connected as citizens, but instead divided by pursuit of capital and security.

Thus, we should not be surprised when our politicians deceive us; they are only doing what is necessary to advance themselves by the modern rules: every man for himself-*dog eat dog*. They can rarely have true concern for the collective mass of people, because from birth they were told *their fellow citizen was their completion.* So there is no true connection to the people, just hollowed words used to manipulate and advance themselves.

Higher up the modern aristocrat ladder and a much more guilty party are the merchants. Under their rule life has been reduced to consumerism, material worship, hedonism, and spiritual nihilism. Man's primitive urges and desires are the low hanging fruit that the merchants are constantly picking at. Our lower instincts of instant gratification, lust, greed, gluttony are exploited to the extremes by the modern day merchant class. Their only concern is making money... not our well-being, not our health, not our advancement. Everywhere you go you are reminded of a call to 'instant gratification', be it sex, food, drugs, and/or alcohol...etc. it is shoved in your face every time you turn on the TV, log onto the internet, or go for a walk or drive within the city.

The excuse for this from the merchants is typically 'we are just providing what people want'. This is only half true. Of course people want it, just like a child wants to eat candy all day, but would any sane parent that gave a damn about their child actually encourage them and allow them to eat candy all day? *Of course not.* The truth of the matter is, they (merchants) encourage the demand through advertisement. They see the low hanging fruit and they must have it. Contrast that to people of nobility of the past. For better or worse, they at the very least never encouraged the plebs to disconnect from their neighbors and gluttonously feed their vices.

This is why the merchants also encourage this spiritual nihilism we see growing in the modern day. If you have deeper spiritual beliefs, you are less likely to be wholly consumed with vice, material worship, selfishness and greed. And believe me that's the last thing they want: a human mentally, spiritually and physically healthy...That is the dreaded light to the cockroach! They thrive in the dark where you are at your weakest.

Our modern day set-up is truly a system of divide and conquer... Instead of using the limited resources on Earth to advance humanity, advance understanding of self and surrounding. We allow individuals to horde it, and dispense it back to us in a manner of material lust.

As a people we are at a cross roads for what our future holds...it's *Idiocracy* or *Star Trek*, or in other words it's a dumbed down divided mass pursuing their own personal gratifications, or a structured unified society pursuing great goals. Just to give a quick synopsis for those who have not seen of or heard of the movie *Idiocracy*... It's a comedy about a dystopic future, altho everyone in the future is too damn ignorant to realize it is a dystopia they are living in... The plot of the story is: The U.S government sends a totally average, in every way, guy into the future using a cryogenics chamber... In this future, *which very well could be our own*, the people with low IQ's have massively out bred the people with higher IQs resulting in a world of dummies...actually technological dummies, they have the benefit of the technology left behind by the smart innovators that created them, but with no know how on why or how these things work...They just know they work and make life easier... So long story short, this average guy goes to this dumbed down future and he turns out to be a genius compared to the people of the future. These shit for brains of the future are only concerned with what 'feels good' or what makes them happy....Sound familiar? Star trek on the other hand is a future of a unified structured society, which is fueled by science, rationalism, and questing the unknown universe... Exploring the unknown space, just as thousands of years ago the bravest explored the unknown seas... it's The Faustian spirit manifest.

As of today in 2016 we are rapidly heading towards *Idiocracy*... We are in the age of the google intellectual...Anytime you argue with someone online you can almost hear them run to google and search answers to fit their confirmation bias.

The process of true self-learning has seemed to be lost on the majority of people today...People seem to be more concerned with simply 'just convincing themselves they are right' despite being factually wrong in reality, or like their food, they want their knowledge...fast.... This shows a lack of critical thinking abilities and a fragile ego... A toxic combination when it comes to discussing ideas, or events in present, and history... Peoples lack in ability to admit they are wrong, or seek more objective truths, or even take the time to acquire

45

deep knowledge on a topic is not a result of low IQ, but of societal and cultural influence of modernity where quick, feel good ignorant answers are in vogue. This can be fixed in a structured society...But what is truly alarming and much less reversible is the declining average IQ of humans ...Altho a global epidemic, I'll stay focused on my country : America...Higher IQ people breed less, and lower people breed more...Not my opinion but an observed and documented fact... Also, and this is my opinion because I haven't seen or looked for data on it, but it seems plausible that, with the YOLO mentality, and 'do what feels good' philosophy you have people having more frequent sex with more frequent partners, instead of using virtues to control physical desires and find partners with the most intellectual and emotional commonalties. Unless we take the reins of society and bring this current path of individualism to a complete halt, we are destined to lead our children and their children's children into a regressive society.

World population explosion... Let's say, modern humans have been around for 10,000 years...Could be a lot more, or even less, but the general point is the same...in 1960 the world pop was in the 3 billion...it took 10,000 years to reach 3 billion... today in 2016, the world pop is estimated over 7 billion...that an increase of 4 billion in just 50 years! About a billion each decade! More people and lower IQ not a good combination...Now never mind the massive pollution on this Earth from all these people, what about our resources? They are dwindling... Not only from our use but the use of feeding the animals that we eat! The documentary *Cowspiracy* , puts forth some scary numbers on not only the pollution done by things like cow farts, but the amount of resources we spend on feed the animals themselves... Now 'Cowspiracy' is without doubt vegan propaganda, BUT, even if they exaggerated some of the numbers, even if half of what they claimed is true (which more than half is) it paints a scary picture for our future as a species that lives off the planet... I would highly recommend anyone that watches this video also watch *Cowspiracy* and look into it for yourself...you won't be happy with what you find.

So while IQ declines, population grows, resources dwindle, you would think our attention as a species would be focused on these massive problems? Of course not... You have crazy genius out there like Aubrey de Grey, who are actively seeking to extend human life span through science, he is a part of the Methuselah Foundation ... The whole point of this foundation is to use biology to extend not only healthy life in humans but life itself in humans... And there is nothing more sad then seeing them have to beg for donations... You would think this would be a easy cause for people to get behind...After all they sent how much money to Haiti(in 2010 after the massive earthquake)? But no, of course not, a quick look at Methuselah Foundation twitter followers will show you they have only 4,345... meanwhile big assed Kim has 45.3 million. This is where the *liberated peoples* of modern democracies collective heads are focused on. And the only rebuttal to our problems I have heard is: *don't worry when the time comes we will just figure out another source of energy…* That's around the same level of don't worry Jesus is coming back one day to set things straight…Sorry I can't be satisfied with kicking the can down the road hoping for miracles to happen.

 I still have hope for our country, because I know we are where we are today because people have been molded to be the way they are today. People have been fooled by these terms *"liberty"* and *"Freedom"*…They think having access to 6 million porn sites is freedom, they think having fast food and liquor stores on every corner is a result of liberty…These people have been swindled by abstract terms… No matter what - you are part of a structured system, be it nature, or your surroundings… Why are you more concerned with the size of a girl's ass than great scientific goals? Because you have been conditioned to… Your *"free markets"* created monopolies that attacked the weakest part of the human make-up...Our primal urges... It's the low hanging fruit that the capitalist loves to pick... Because we have been reduced to mere consumers the international business oligarchies have no concern for our mental and physical well-being, their only concern is profit...this is the system we deserve, because we tolerate it. But, I believe things are changing... We have had our fun in hedonism and nihilism...Our collective subconscious is starting to surface, and it is asking for more out of our lives then just simply working buying and dying... That *Faustian spirit* that takes whatever measures necessary to advance is coming to surface. As of today, the loudest voice for an alternative is the modern neo-commies... But that is not a true alterative - that is human slavery... They, like Capitalism, reduce people to soulless numbers...No, **the true alterative is Fascism**...and you can call it what you want...Hell you can call it the *Liberty Freedom 1776 Party*...As long as it has the Fascist principles it will lead us out of the cave lit by neon lights into the light of the might sun...A structured society built around collectivism, science, knowledge, spirituality, brotherhood, traditional gender roles, a quest for understanding and mastering the unknown, a molding of a new man a better man, not a man addicted to big macs and fat asses, but a true over man... No matter what systems we live under we are being molded by our environment; do you want cooperate oligarchies molding you, your children? Or would you prefer fellow citizens who are motivated by Masculine Virtues over capital... So its *Idiocrasy* or *Star Trek* my friends. Which will you choose?

Fascism

&

The New Man

"When a nation rises up ardent to fight for its freedom and honor, it is always a minority that really fires the multitude." — **Oswald Spengler**

If we could simplify and generalize the basic tenets promoted by the 3 major political positions of the modern era they would be as such:

Communism: United we are Equal

Democracy: United we are Individuals

Fascism: United we are Stronger

Now as a mass and a society we can pretty much interpret what "stronger" means... In all civil and martial aspects of society, the society would function with a lot more cohesiveness and achieve measurable results but what does being "stronger" entail to the individual?

When it comes to the individual; what makes the Third position, Fascism, truly unique from the other two political positions of Democracy and Communism is Fascism emphasis on building up the induvial in order to create the best individual period. When a society is judged on results, only the best quality of people can hope to obtain the most achievement... So it benefits the collective to build up the induvial. As some selected Fascist works explain:

Origins and Doctrine of Fascism

"We seek to provoke in the Italian soul an inextinguishable thirst for knowledge that is the labor and reform of the interior of humankind and the acquisition of the moral and material means for a life always more elevated, always more productive, for the individual and for the nation—in fact, for humanity and the world. We seek the enhancement of the world. We seek the enhancement of the world because we live in it and with it."

Fascism seeks to improve the mental and physical aspects of people...say what you want about the Nazis...but there were no fat kids in the Hitler youth. Compare that to today, where obesity has become an epidemic amongst our youth... Now tell me which government cares more for its people? The answer lies in the facts.

For My Legionaries

"This country is dying of lack of men, not of lack of programs; at least this is our opinion. That, in other words, it is not programs that we must have, but men, new men, For such as people are today, formed by politicians and infected by the Judaic influence, they will compromise the most brilliant political programs. This kind of man who is alive today in Romanian politics we earlier met in history. Nations died under his rule and states collapsed. The greatest wrong done to us by Jews and the political system,

the greatest national danger to which they exposed us, is neither the grabbing of the Romanian soil and subsoil, nor even the tragic annihilation of the Romanian middle class, nor the great number of Jews in our schools, professions, etc. and not even the influence they exercise over our political life-though each of these in itself is a mortal danger for our people. The greatest national peril is the fact that they have deformed, disfigured our Daco-Romanic racial structure, giving birth to this type of man, creating this human refuse, this moral failure.. the politician who has nothing in common with the nobility of our race anymore; who dishonors and kills us, If this species of man continues to 'lead this country, the Romanian people will close its eyes forever and Romania will collapse, in spite of all the brilliant programs with which the "trickery" of this degenerate creature is able to dazzle the eyes of the unfortunate multitudes. From among all the pests brought to us by the Jewish invasion, this is the most frightening one!"

Humans are adaptable creatures and highly susceptible to suggestion. If you don't believe that, then you are severely mis-informed. Everything from our races, to our cultures has come from adaption and suggestion in one form or another... So when a society permits the promotion of vice, then that will be what the society descends in to, and likewise when a society promotes virtue that's what a society ascends to... Fascist philosophy knows this and this is why promotion of building up the induvial and promoting heathy virtues amongst citizens is taken seriously...Oversight of media and industry is to ensure that the large majority of entertainment and information benefit the individual and not hinder him. Unlike today where your lower self is exploited for Capitalist profit.

Robert Brassilach

"Fascism is a spirit. For us it is not a political doctrine, nor is it an economic doctrine. It was first of all an anti-conformist, anti- bourgeois spirit, in which disrespect plays its part. It is a spirit opposed to

prejudices- to class prejudices, (as well) as to others. It is the very spirit of friendship, which we (will) have (desired) to have raised to the level of the friendship of the whole nation. A new civilization—A new human type being born- the fascist man and woman."

Ubiratan Pimentel

"The superman will have to be one who is not doubted. His words must speak volumes of verifiable truth. He will have to be, without any doubts, a man of unquestionable principle; a personage who's statements are without question. He will be the profound fountainhead of wisdom to which all citizens may come to for accurately succinct and worthy responses...The integral man is the 'superman' of Nietzsche; it is the total man, the ethical man, the top man, the new man...The superman is the maximum exultation of the inner revolutionary self as well as unbridled action."

Fascism seeks to create this new man through philosophical, scientific, spiritual, and physical revival... Oversight of education, and of media is crucial for this...This Fascist oversight is often attacked by both liberals and conservatives, but their alternative is to have corporate oligarchies control the narrative of the people and as we have seen, all these oligarchs care about is the accumulating more capital and more power at the expense of the citizens wellbeing. So when the options are: influence from cooperate oligarchies or a government that seeks fantastic unified goals from a competent people, well that's no decision at all as far as I am concerned.

The government serves as are parental figure heads... Now think about your own parent or if you are apparent your own children...would you think it more beneficial to feed your kids a constant flow of soda and candy or of water and spinach? If you gave a single fuck about your kids you would give them the water and spinach over the soda and candy...Fascism is that water and spinach.... Today our government feeds us junk food, junk television and junk education... because of that we have become junk people... The Fascist philosophy seeks to change that...Today we have no Fascist government around to help us become better, so the Fascist, the real believer must take it upon himself to improve himself the best he can...Because until you take on the battle with yourself you will not be fit to take on the battle of society in an effective manner... Fascism is more than a political orientation. It is a way of life and it demands you at your highest potential.

The best you benefits me.

The best you benefits my kids.

The best you benefits my neighborhood.

The best you benefits our nation.

Our personal improvements directly translates to our collective improvements... for that reason Fascist oversight exists to help mold the best you...Nature was given to you at birth but nurture...nurture is in the hands of the positive Fascist society.

Economy

*"For even if the good of the community coincides with that of the individual, it is clearly a greater and more perfect thing to achieve and preserve that of a community; for while it is desirable to secure what is good in the case of an individual, to do so in the case of the people or state is something finer and more sublime". - **Aristotle**

Quotes taken from '**The Economic Foundations of Fascism**' by. Paul Einzig

"In its social aspects, Fascism endeavors to conciliate the conflicting interests of the different classes. It does not aim at eliminating class distinctions; on the contrary, it seeks to maintain them with their special characteristics, and to obtain collaboration between them."

"While in the sphere of distribution the Fascist economic system has discarded individualism to a great extent, in the sphere of production individual initiative still plays, and will always play, a prominent part."

"The complete elimination of individual initiative is calculated to reduce the efficiency of production to such an extent as to deprive mankind of the benefits of an improved system of distribution. At one extreme there is pure Capitalism with its production stimulated to the extreme by the moving force of

unhampered individual interests, and with its hopelessly inadequate system of distribution, which results in periodic crises that deprive even the privileged classes of the benefit of technical progress. At the other extreme there is Communism, with its system of distribution which approaches the ideal, and with its system of production which, while benefiting by planning, has the fatal handicap of lack of individual initiative. Between the two extremes there is Fascism, whose system of production benefits by planning, though not to the same extent as under Communism, and benefits by individual initiative, though perhaps to a somewhat less extent than in countries of laissez-faire, and with a system of distribution which, while inferior to that of Communism, may become infinitely superior to that of pure Communism, may become infinitely superior to that of pure Capitalism."

"Socialism, carried to its logical conclusion as Communism, aims at complete equality of incomes; Fascism does not contemplate going so far. While endeavoring to secure for the working classes their

fair share of the proceeds of production, Fascism wishes to retain the benefits of the incentive to individualistic production represented by profit-earning possibilities. It aims at preventing the earning of excessive profits at the expense of the working classes."

Fascism does not try to equalize people like Communism, or to divide people like Capitalism, but much like Aristotle's 'mean ethics' Fascism seek the virtuous middle ground. Class exists, personal incentive exists, but the differences between people are shortened. Citizens are brought closer together…For instance; let's say the pay scale of A to Z exists…Where **Z** was the most money a citizen could make a year and **A** was the least a citizen could make. **Z** would not be billions of dollars, (like it is today) and **A** would not a homeless person (like it is today) Instead **Z** would be plentiful enough to enjoy their wealth…Their earned wealth…Earned being the important part… Not speculated or swindled. And **A** would be sufficient enough to provide a living. Bring the pay gap closer together harms no one, but helps everyone.

"Differences arising between employers and employees are settled by conciliation, or, should that fail, by the decision of special Labour Courts to which they have to be submitted, and whose judgment is binding on both parties"

"It is only when, in the opinion of the authorities, private activity is not in accordance with national interest that they decide to intervene. This intervention may be either active or passive. If the government considers that in a certain direction individual initiative does not adequately meet requirements, it will intervene to stimulate production in that particular branch."

No longer with employee and employer be riddled with battles of self-interest. But rather an oversight by Fascist government members will intervene, when needed, to settle disputes…Having loyalty not to the workers or owners but to the society as a whole.

"The Government will, however, always be ready to intervene in cases of cut-throat competition. A producer can lower his sale prices provided that the reduction is the result of some new invention, or of the application of more efficient methods. But if he tries to ruin his rivals by selling at a loss until they are eliminated from the field, the authorities do not hesitate to take preventive action."

"The main object of the Corporate State is the planning of production and the determination of distribution in accordance with changing requirements."

The idea of a planned, or rather largely planned economy is often attacked by economic "experts". And their wonderful answer is always: *'our personal greed is the best motivator for economy.* This madness has kept the capitalist wheel rolling far too long.

"It has become part of a system in which both employers and employees have to submit their individual interests to the common good."

"In the Corporate State economic initiative is left in private hands; it is supplemented by State intervention only if and when private initiative is considered inadequate to serve public interests."

"In addition to supplementing individual initiative when it is considered inadequate to serve the requirements of public interest, the Fascist regime aims at guiding it, both positively and negatively. Its object is to prevent private initiative from working against public interest, and to stimulate its activities in accordance with public interest."

"It is not merely the fear of punishment that prevents a great majority of bankers from disregarding the decision of their Corporation, but also the knowledge that their rivals will observe the same rules."

The life blood of today's economy is feeding off of people primal desires... The Fascist economy does not feed off of the citizen, but is a tool of the citizen. A tool used to enhance life, business, growth, and gain...To serve the common good, not the few.

Why Fascism

"If two irreconcilable elements are struggling with each other, the solution lies in force. There has never been any other solution in history, and there never will be." – **Benito Mussolini**

With our planet resources dwindling, and a divided population growing, it is time for us to take a moment to ponder: *what are we doing and why are we doing it?* Just because we were born into a system of government and a way of life does not mean we are destined to be decisionless about our path in life. Life is short and we are ever evolving, we have to be honest with ourselves: *We are wasting our short time and our potential as a unified, driven, focused people.* Instead of working together to learn, explore, discover and advance - we are working against each other, for material objects and capital that amounts to nothing but numbers in your bank account. Instead of spending our time working towards a cause and goals that brings us all together, we instead spend the lion's share of our time occupied with fulfilling instant self-gratification desires. And for why? You can't take it with you...As they say. A *tale* about Alexander the greats last days explains it best:

The Three Final Wishes of Alexander

"Alexander was a great Greek king. As a military commander, he was undefeated and the most successful throughout history. On his way home from conquering many countries, he came down with an illness. At that moment, his captured territories, powerful army, sharp swords, and wealth all had no meaning to him. He realized that death would soon arrive and he would be unable to return to his homeland. He told his officers: "I will soon leave this world. I have three final wishes. You need to carry out what I tell you." His generals, in tears, agreed.

"My first wish is to have my physician bring my coffin home alone. After a gasping for air, Alexander continued: "My second wish is scatter the gold, silver, and gems from my treasure-house along the path to the tomb when you ship my coffin to the grave." After wrapping in a woolen blanket and resting for a while, he said: "My final wish it to put my hands outside the coffin." People surrounding him all were very curious, but no one dare to ask the reason. Alexander's most favored general kissed his hand and asked: "My Majesty, We will follow your instruction. But can you tell us why you want us to do it this way?" After taking a deep breath, Alexander said: "I want *everyone to understand the three lessons I have learned. To let my physician carry my coffin alone is to let people realize that a physician cannot really cure people's illness. Especially when they face death, the physicians are powerless. I hope people will learn to treasure their lives. My second wish is to tell people not to be like me in pursuing wealth. I spent my whole life pursuing wealth, but I was wasting my time most of the time. My third wish to let people understand that I came to this world in empty hands and I will leave this world also in empty hands." he closed his eyes after finished talking and stopped breathing.*

If the moral of the story dawns on you, I ask why are we wasting our lives in materialist hedonism?

If we can master our *will* we can obtain the *power* to change the direction of Mankind. *We are not molded by destiny - we mold destiny.* It's a simple solution, but there is nothing simple about actually applying it to reality.

We have forgotten, or been distracted from the reality that we take for granted every day and that reality is: **Our every living conscious moment is a wonderful miracle in itself!** It's fucking amazing. I am continually in awe of it. For shame, we waste this miracle! We allowed the *merchants* and *lawyers* to help us forget this miracle...To simplify life to our basic primitive desires; to pacify ourselves in indulgence. Because we have done this, we are now a people that will accept insult; we are willing to work jobs with no purpose outside providing capital which in turn pays for food, home, car, fun... This *miracle* being reduced to: **work, buy, die, repeat.**

This is what our modern Liberal Capitalistic Democracy has brought us. This is how you will spend your short ride on this rock, IF, that is the life you are willing to accept.

Fascism seeks to combat this and create a life and system towards unity, common goals, a common good, and advancement. Life with purpose...Real purpose, not a purpose that can be manufactured on an assembly line, but that true feeling of purpose that fills your soul...Something not bought, or given, but born within. Determined, disciplined, and unified, we can achieve this.

The 'modern' Fascist

*"The first and greatest victory is to conquer yourself; to be conquered by yourself is of all things most shameful and vile."- **Plato***

What can the modern Fascist do? Well the last thing you need to do is join some useless internet "Fascist party". Most of these "parties" are nothing more the voyeurism and role playing. Since (currently) there are no Fascist parties worth joining, what can be done is (1) Self-improvement and (2) Get involved in local politics, or with your community and preach Fascist values.

Our battle is to aspire to live up to our ideals. We must be healthy in body, mind, and soul if we are to reach our fellow citizens with the good message of Fascism. If we are physically out of shape, or hate ourselves - or hate people in general, we will not be good ambassadors to our fellow citizens...We must truly care for our fellow citizens, and view them as potential brothers and sisters...No matter how hostile some of them may be to the good word of Fascism, we must truly be coming from a good place when we seek to convert them. You must remember they were raised to hate, fear, and attack the very thought of the word "Fascism". Only by you being a truly decent person...A true Fascist, will you be able to reach our fellow misguided kin.

We have all been raised in this modern gutter...To live up to our ideals we will have to do a lot of self-breaking down and then building back up...We must become our very own personal boot camp... Playing both roles: drill instructor and grunt. Discover and use methods to regain control of yourself, something like the "8 steps to higher evolution"

1. Idealism and Self-Discipline

Idealism being the belief in something greater, a goal in life that extends outside of yourself. Is there anything metaphysical that you're a truly willing to die for? Go hungry for? Live uncomfortably for? Sacrifice for? Probably not...When you evaluate your values how high is your idealism? Idealism is our much need fuel of irrationalism that thrusts our rationalist selves forward into chaos...And Chaos brings about change. The nihilist has nothing to live for, but the idealist has everything to kill for. Our fanatical love of the metaphysical ideals is crucial to manifesting *Thought* into *Action*. Make no mistake, The search for true idealism is no easy task; much too often people pick ideals like they do a pair of shoes... you must discover a belief that invokes real reaction within you...real enough to have it consume your life. Where taking the ideal from the *meta* and bringing to the physical becomes obsession. Self-discipline being the key to everything good in you, a control of your emotions, passions, weaknesses. A true mastering and control of yourself. Discipline is the closest thing you can achieve to real freedom... With discipline you are free from your lower instincts which bind you with primitive urges. Discipline is like a muscle the more you say no - the more it grows. But discipline is not found in the absolute or the abstinence but rather in the moderation like Aristotle's ethics... To completely indulge yourself is lack of self-control, but to completely abstain is a fear of one's self...Discipline is found in the happy medium. True control of self. Through discipline you are free to pursue your higher self... Discipline is the foundation of all self-improvement.

2. Physical and Mental Purity

Do not gorge on Junk food or junk for your mind... If you sabotage yourself by flooding your body with toxins from processed foods or visual toxins from junk television you de-purify body and mind... Your body and mind cannot perform at its highest potential when it is polluted; So that means less Cheetos and soda, more spinach and Chicken; less porn and reality tv and more beneficial reading and self-contemplation... Only by fueling your mind and body properly can you hope to get the best results out of yourself... These harmful but pleasurable sensations found in food and entertainments are provided for you at glutinous proportions because they help restrain you... Break free of the imposed restraints by purifying yourself: If you take care of your body and mind- your body and mind will take care of you.

3. Physical Exercise for Physical Body

A part of purifying your body is strengthening your body through physical exercise. Physical exercise adds self-confidence, over-all heath improvements, longevity in life and is ascetically desired or respected by your peers. Physical exercise is your thought put into direct action. Your body becomes a upgraded vehicle now more effectively used to transport your ideals. Consistency in physical exercise is just one of the many self-battles one must endure through discipline to make themselves a better person. In *Sun & Steel* Yukio Mishima equated the lack of physical masculine aesthetics in modern man as a result of their lack of virtuous masculinity within themselves... They dismiss what is better because they themselves are so far away from better. "The cynicism that regards all hero worship as comical is always shadowed by a sense of physical inferiority." Physical strength is crucial in both the meta and the physical aspects of life, if your body is weak, your will is weak. And if your will is weak, you will remain in the satin bracelets that currently shackle you.

4. Control the Breath and Life Energy

Breath is your life energy - without breath there is no life within you...This life energy is an undefinable force within us that bonds us all to the conscious world. Mastering your breath is mastering yourself and your physiology... Mastering your breath is an ancient knowledge that even today has modern prophets extorting its virtues... There are many different methods and teachings in regards to breath control. Personally I have found favorable results in the *Wim Hoff* breathing methods and nose breathing methods discussed in books like the "Oxygen Advantage" While Wim Hoff's methods and the nasal breathing methods advocated to induce nitric oxide throughout the body in the "oxygen advantage" may contradict each other on surface value. One, being solely focused on nasal breathing the other by breathing by any means necessary. I have found a happy medium that has produced noticeable positive improvement in control of my breath... The pragmatic applications to life with breath control are countless...everything from stressful situations to panicked states and in high pressure moments, all can be altered one way or another through breath. Mastering our breath is getting more in touch with one's self which leads us to our fifth step

5. Interiorization of the senses

"The unexamined life is not worth living" Socrates

Self-contemplation... long silent hours spent in solitude examining one's self. Your behaviors, your habits, your feelings...where, why and how do they come from? Where can you make them take you? I have reached understandings about myself in the sober solitude of my cell or study...I have found answers to myself randomly appearing out of nowhere while high on marijuana or hallucinogens... I cherish every breakthrough...Every one is a peeling back of yet another layer of the seemingly never ending onion that is I... If there is truly someone I have no pity for in this life it is those who do not take the time to explore themselves in hopes to understand themselves and their surroundings better. They are truly not worth living. I could provide quote after quote of great thinkers through human existence on the importance of self-contemplation... many a great man has known we can never become who we aspire to be - if we don't even know who we are. You must come to know yourself... you must at times force yourself into solitude and dive into that abyss that is you... Be aware of who you are so that no man can take advantage of your unawareness. Because people are deficient of inner contemplation they have that void filled with material trinkets supplied by the very bastards that wish to keep you on the hamster wheel of nihilist materialism and servitude.

6. One-Point Concentration

Every self-help book worth a damn will try to neuro-linguistically program you to use mental tricks to rely on to help you improve yourself...one of those mental tricks is "one point concentration" do not over burden yourself with many battles, but slay one dragon at a time, achieve one goal after another...before you can fly you must learn to crawl , walk and run, and you can only do that by focusing on the next step ahead of you -- not looking further down the road in disappointment because of the long path still ahead... Focus-advance-improve and overcome.

7. Cleansing the Subconscious Mind

A cleansing of the subconscious mind will result in a healthier conscious mind...we are often harassed with negativity from within ourselves...that little negative voice that tells us we can't, or we are unworthy...that self-sabotage that always seems to appear when we are doing so good. Quieting and eventually silencing that inner negative can be achieved... Methods like meditation, yoga... Core imaging...self-contemplation, dream interpretation are among some of the ways to address your sub-conscious... How do you know if any of these tools of improvement are working on your subconscious? When that inner negativity goes from a voice to a whisper...when the positive voice becomes the dominate functioning inner dialog, then you know you have addressed and repaired the negativity swirling around your sub-conscious

8. Super Consciousness

This is you at your true potential... Physical, mentally and spiritually in tune with yourself-your surrounding and your idealism...

Now is it mandatory for all 8 steps to be mastered before change manifests in the world? Of course not... The climb to a better you is a never ending ascent that is often met with a stumble here and there, but as long as you get back up and continue the climb – you continue to strive for a better you and a better world. As Yukio Mishima said in Runaway Horses: *"To be thus a man was to give constant proof of one's manliness–to be more a man today than yesterday, more a man tomorrow than today. To be a man was to forge ever upward toward the peak of manhood, there to die amid the white snows of that peak."* Simply acknowledging your faults, weakness and lower self is enough to get you going in the right direction, and is enough to set the wheel of change in motion...But, to deny your faults, ignore your weakness and indulge your lower self and fool yourself into believing you have already reached the peak. Then it is here at your peak that you will remain.

Steps like the '8 steps', or any of the other numerous methods that can be used to better yourself- must be implemented. The only way we will be able to change the world is if we first master ourselves. We must be willing to set the example.

This next decade will determine the path of our country, and possibly the world, for generations to come. We are at a moment in time when opportunity is there, the door is open... who will walk through it? The modern neo Marxist liberals or the modern Fascists? Capitalism has started to decay, what comes next could be something much worse, or something far better, what it is is only *up to us to act.*